£1-49

13

C000068264

Weekend Breaks

A play

John Godber

Samuel French — London
New York - Toronto - Hollywood

© 1998 BY JOHN GODBER

Rights of Performance by Amateurs are controlled by Samuel French Ltd, 52 Fitzroy Street, London W1P 6JR, and they, or their authorized agents, issue licences to amateurs on payment of a fee. **It is an infringement of the Copyright to give any performance or public reading of the play before the fee has been paid and the licence issued.**

The Royalty Fee indicated below is subject to contract and subject to variation at the sole discretion of Samuel French Ltd.

       Basic fee for each and every
           performance by amateurs   Code M
           in the British Isles

The Professional Rights in this play are controlled by ALAN BRODIE REPRESENTATION, 211 Piccadilly, London, W1V 9LD

The publication of this play does not imply that it is necessarily available for performance by amateurs or professionals, either in the British Isles or Overseas. Amateurs and professionals considering a production are strongly advised in their own interests to apply to the appropriate agents for written consent before starting rehearsals or booking a theatre or hall.

ISBN 0 573 01940 1

Please see page iv for further copyright information

WEEKEND BREAKS

Weekend Breaks was first performed by Hull Truck Theatre Company at the Alhambra Theatre, Bradford on 19th May, 1997 with the following cast:

Martin Dawson	Nicholas Lane
Len Dawson	Dicken Ashworth
Joan Dawson	Judi Jones

Directed by John Godber
Assistant Zoe Seaton

Subsequently produced at the West Yorkshire Playhouse with the following cast:

Martin Dawson	Adrian Hood
Len Dawson	Dicken Ashworth
Joan Dawson	Judi Jones

COPYRIGHT INFORMATION

(See also page ii)

This play is fully protected under the Copyright Laws of the British Common-wealth of Nations, the United States of America and all countries of the Berne and Universal Copyright Conventions.

All rights including Stage, Motion Picture, Radio, Television, Public Reading, and Translation into Foreign Languages, are strictly reserved.

No part of this publication may lawfully be reproduced in ANY form or by any means — photocopying, typescript, recording (including video-recording), manuscript, electronic, mechanical, or otherwise—or be transmitted or stored in a retrieval system, without prior permission.

Licences for amateur performances are issued subject to the understanding that it shall be made clear in all advertising matter that the audience will witness an amateur performance; that the names of the authors of the plays shall be included on all programmes; and that the integrity of the authors' work will be preserved.

The Royalty Fee is subject to contract and subject to variation at the sole discretion of Samuel French Ltd.

In Theatres or Halls seating Four Hundred or more the fee will be subject to negotiation.

In Territories Overseas the fee quoted above may not apply. A fee will be quoted on application to our local authorized agent, or if there is no such agent, on application to Samuel French Ltd, London.

VIDEO-RECORDING OF AMATEUR PRODUCTIONS

Please note that the copyright laws governing video-recording are extremely complex and that it should not be assumed that any play may be video-recorded for whatever purpose without first obtaining the permission of the appropriate agents. The fact that a play is published by Samuel French Ltd does not indicate that video rights are available or that Samuel French Ltd controls such rights.

CHARACTERS

Martin Dawson, mid thirties
Len Dawson, his father; late sixties
        (also playing late thirties)
Joan Dawson, his mother; late sixties
        (also playing late thirties)

A Voice (page 1 only)

The action takes place on a large empty stage

Time — the present

PUBLISHER'S NOTE

To avoid repetition in the stage directions, passages in which Martin's speech is addressed direct to the audience have been indicated the first time only. This direction refers to the whole section until informed otherwise.

Chapter 2

ACT I

A large empty stage. The stage floor is painted black. Nothing is on stage except two black dining chairs

The House Lights and preset fade to Black-out

We hear a voice

Voice Ladies and gentlemen, welcome to the *Comedy Club*, and a big welcome to tonight's first-timer. He is a Doctor of Comedy, a Master of Arsing about, a Bachelor of Soup. Ladies and gentlemen, the *Comedy Club* is proud to present — The anxious comedy ramblings of Dr Martin Dawson!

There is a short burst of music

Dr Martin Dawson (Mart), a dry and slightly uninspiring man in his mid-thirties comes on stage. He stands c, acknowledges the audience and commences a comedy routine. His delivery is very easy, and he is instantly likeable. We notice that he is dressed in a smart suit with casual wear

He is caught in a spotlight, as he will be throughout when he is performing his act

Mart (*to the audience*) I hate flying. I do. They have to put me in a crate to get me up. They have to back me on like a donkey, blinkered, drugged mostly. Completely comatose. L A, eleven hours! Insane. I'd rather be buried alive. No, I mean it. I like soil. I went there once to hawk a film script. LA I mean, not soil. Eleven hours on a plane. Eight hours, and I need a shit. I haven't moved in eight hours. I'm sat there, I don't want to move in case I upset the balance of the plane or something. There's these kids walking about. I want 'em to sit down. Everytime the bing-bong thing comes on, I'm having a stroke. I think we're going down. Bing-bong; oh, we're down. Bing-bong; this is it. I'm that tense, I've doubled my own body weight. I mean I am actually flying the plane. Without my complete mental concentration the thing is going to drop anyway. I'm nipping my arse that bad that I've got cramp in my sphincter! I have to stand up on a plane. It's my first time. I don't like standing up in public, but on a plane it seems absurd.

So I'm sat in the bog in the dark, 'cos I don't know that when you lock the door the light comes on. So I'm sat in the dark thinking, shit, a brand new plane and the light's gone in the bog. Argh! And then it comes over the tannoy, bing-bong, "Please fasten your seat belts, we are going through a sand storm". Sand storm? Seat belts? I'm on the bog in the dark. I spent six years at university. I thought sand was supposed to be in the desert? Couldn't go. No, complete and utter shut down in the roughage department. Couldn't go in fact, until I'm pitching this film plot to Warner Bros, and then I can't stop going. Everytime I get to a new twist in the tale, whooph, "excuse me" and I'm in there. It was the first film pitch they'd ever heard being shouted to them from the bog.

No, flying, I tell you, unnatural. I went on this "Fear of Flying" course. They send you up in a plane with three hundred sorry souls all of whom are shit-scared of the old aerial experience. It's like *Cuckoo's Nest* in the sky. They bring on these two pilots. And I'm sat sweating nervously. And the guy says, he'd like to introduce us to the two Stews, right, because these guys are both called Stew. Now he thinks this is a joke. I think he's said, they'd like to welcome us to the two students. Oh man, unfair sending us in the sky with two complete novices.

But my mam and dad love it. They can't get enough of it. They fly all over the place. They've got these Air Miles. No good to me at all. I'm waiting for "Bus Miles" yeh. Or "East Coast Rail Service Miles." Or "Walk Miles". Yeh, they love it, fly all over. Well Spain mostly, well Málaga actually. The Costa del Sol. They're a great source of material. You can keep your Zolas and Becketts. These two are a living breathing example of absurd naturalism. They deserve an entire literary movement of their own. In fact they're the reason I'm up here. No in fact that's not true. They should be up here, they should, they're funnier than me. Mind you that's not so hard tonight. They're the funniest people I have ever met, but the thing is they don't know it!

Music plays softly underneath

During this sequence Len appears US. *He is a large man in his late sixties. He has a small travelling bag. He stands frozen in a spotlight*

Len Bloody clutch is playing me up, I think the gear-box is slipping. I can't afford a new'un. I've told your mam if she wants a new car she'll have to go out on the streets. She says, "What do you want, a new car or a new bike?" I says, by the look of you these days we'd be lucky to get a pogo-stick. All right then? Long time no see. Still look the same then?

Mart I hadn't seen them for six months. We had a lot of catching up to do.

Len Lost some weight maybe?

Mart That was a big conversation between me and him.

Len Your mam's just coming.

Mart I'm going back a year now, right. I was staying up in the Lakes at a cottage I'd hired. I was working on a screenplay.

Len Traffic's bloody murder out there.

Mart I mean it's not that I was a writer or anything, right? I was teaching theatre studies at Humberside University.

Len She's driving me bloody mad, your mother.

Mart He's letting her struggle up the stairs. She's bad on her feet. He'll be getting his own back for some domestic warfare that's obviously broken out in the car ride up here.

Len Her feet are getting worse, and her bloody nerves.

Mart He knows all this but he doesn't bother to help her. (*To Len*) Nothing's changed then?

Len Eh?

Mart Still complaining about her.

Len You know us. What a bloody drive!

Mart You've made good time though.

Len Ay not bad. Six and a half hours.

Mart (*to the audience*) They had set off at nine that morning. It usually takes my dad three times as long to go anywhere as it actually need take.

Len We got up at five. You know what your mother's like.

Mart When they go to Spain they set off the day before the day they're supposed to set off. In case they meet anything on the way to the airport. Like Martians or something. 'Cos they have a lot of martians around East Midlands airport.

Joan enters. She too is in her late sixties. She is rather more delicate on her feet. She has a small bag

Joan Your dad just leaves me, he's not bothered. I could get bloody mugged or anything. As long as he's got the car parked he's not bothered about anybody else.

Mart Ah joy!

Joan And I don't know why you had to come all the way up here.

Mart My mam? Always complaining. It's like everything is a problem.

Joan I nearly broke my neck on them steps out there.

Mart I reckon when I was born she looked at me and said, "I don't know why you had to be born. It's such a bloody effort."

Joan And my feet... ?

Mart has become embroiled in the reality of the situation

Mart (*to Joan*) My dad said they were bad. Well come in then. Let's get you
  sorted.
Joan We couldn't find you.
Mart Well you've found me now!
Joan About time.
Mart (*to the audience*) I'd rented a place and I thought. Good idea. Let's get
  my mam and dad up for a weekend break, it'll do 'em good. In any case
  they're good source material, aren't they?
Joan What a journey. I don't know why you couldn't come and write in the
  spare bedroom like you used to.
Mart The Lakes are inspirational. My bedroom's a shoe box.
Joan Fancy coming all the way up here. It's just a waste of petrol.
Len Six hours, not bad, that, you know.
Mart Aren't you going to say hallo then?
Joan Why should I? We're here, aren't we? What do you want me to do?
Mart Well, a kiss or a shake of hands is the customary greeting.
Joan Oh I can't be doing with all that stuff.
Mart Or a simple: Hallo, Martin, how are you?
Joan Have you heard him? He's always got to have you doing something
  stupid.
Mart I thought you might have changed but ——
Len You'll never change your mam, you should know that by now.
Joan He'll not change me.
Len Bloody roads. There's road works all the way from Doncaster.
Joan Ay and we must have hit every pot-hole.
Len Bloody roads.
Joan That's your dad's driving. He's getting worse.
Mart You had a good trip then?
Joan I feel as sick as a dog.
Len The heater's overheating on the car. And we couldn't put the window
  down because of the rain.
Joan And my back's killing me, and your dad's ears are playing him up.
Mart Not too good then?
Joan It took him fifteen goes to pass his test. And I still don't think he's
  passed it properly. I hate riding with him.
Len I have passed my test.
Joan I still think he hasn't passed it.
Len I have.
Joan He's the worst bloody driver in Christendom.
Len I have passed my test you know.

A beat

Joan Cold in here isn't it?

Len I'm all right.

Joan No central heating is there, Martin?

Mart No, they didn't have it in 1850. We could burn some old clothes or something later. Then I'll put a rabbit on the spit.

Joan I don't know if I'll be able to sleep if it's this cold.

Mart If you get too bad, we can put another blanket on the bed. There's a fan heater, we can put that on.

Joan I can't get warm; I think I must have thin blood.

Len I sometimes wonder if she's got any blood at all.

Joan Kids aren't with you, then?

Mart No.

Joan Oh, I thought they might be.

Len Nice little cottage. I bet it's cold in winter.

Mart I bet it's cold in summer.

Joan I thought we might have seen them.

Mart Just me, Mam, I'm afraid. But I can go if you want. Just leave me on my own. Again!

Joan Not seen 'em for ages, have we? I talked to Martha, but when did we last see 'em?

Len Not seen 'em for ages, have we?

Joan Everything all right?

Mart Yeh, they're fine.

Joan Are they at home?

Mart No, no, April's left them with Pam and Don this weekend. She's gone away on a course thing.

Joan Well they could've come up here then.

Len We'd've kept them out of your way.

Mart I've come up here to work. I mean I'm behind with the deadline as it is.

Joan Well, we can go if you want.

Len We've only just got here.

Joan Well, if he's busy.

Mart No, I'm only saying — it's just that they are wanting a lot of changes and I need to do them.

Len They tell you to change things do they?

Mart Yeh, they have a script developer.

Len I thought it was your idea?

Mart Well it is, but you've got to have input.

Len I wouldn't have that. If it was my idea I'd tell 'em to stick it.

Mart It doesn't work quite like that, Dad. They've come up with some good
   ideas.
Len Ay, but it's no longer yours, is it?
Joan I mean, I've never liked the Lake District anyway. Never have. The last
   time we came up here — when was it?
Len Thirteen years ago.
Joan Thirteen years ago.
Len Thirteen years ago.
Mart Was it?
Joan The last time we came up here was thirteen years ago.
Len (*to Joan*) Your Mabel came.
Joan We came with our Mabel.
Len It rained.
Joan It rained all week, didn't it?
Len All week.
Joan I haven't been to the Lakes since.
Len I don't mind the Lakes.
Joan I hate it.
Len Your mam hates the Lakes.
Joan It comes in on me. I think it's the hills. And the roads. All the roads are
   windy, aren't they? Thirteen years ago when we came with our Mabel.
Len A lot of water's passed under the bridge since then.
Joan Yeh, I mean we were both well then.
Len Thirteen years ago and we came up with your Aunt Mabel.
Joan Dead now, you know?
Mart I went to the funeral.
Len Thirteen years.

A beat

Mart How are you then?
Joan Dropping to bits.
Len I'm all right.
Joan He's not as good as he was, his angina gets to him, doesn't it?
Len My angina ——
Joan — gets to him.
Len I can't get about like I could.
Joan I have to carry all the shopping when we go to Sainsbury's.
Len I'm all right though.
Joan He's all right. But he can't lift anything, can you?
Len I have to make do.
Joan We both have to make do.
Len I make do.

Joan No, I've never liked the Lakes. Why didn't you go to the seaside?

Mart You'll enjoy it in the morning. It's a lovely view from the back, you can see right across the lake.

Joan Have you had your tablet?

Len I've had it.

Joan He's got a tablet for every part of his body now.

Len Ay, I'm like the six million dollar man. I'm made out of tablets.

Joan He can't get stressed out.

Mart Well, that's why you're here, there's no need to get stressed out, is there?

Joan It's a pity we're not going to see the kids, isn't it? I thought they might have come, I was looking forward to that.

Len Oh ay, I'm on tablets now! Blood pressure and angina, and one for my nerves.

Mart (*to the audience*)There are two reasons why he is bad with his nerves. One is working down the pit for thirty years and the other one is living with my mam. He says he makes all the big decisions in their life. Like what shall we do with nuclear waste? And my mam makes all the small decisions, like what they watch on TV and what time will they go to bed? So, an hour later me and my dad are stood outside looking at the shimmering beauty of the lake. And me mam's sat inside listening to some music. She doesn't come out because the fresh air makes her ears bleed, or something.

Music plays softly underneath

Mart is joined by Len as Joan freezes US. *A dappled gobo to create lakeside garden*

Len I like it up here, kid. It's just that we're both under the weather at the moment.

Mart (*to Len*) Well, just relax this weekend.

Len Your mam's not been so well.

Mart Why, what's up with her?

Len I think it's her nerves, playing her up.

Mart Again.

Len Ay, she's complaining of aches all over the place.

Mart What's the doctor said?

Len He's sick of seeing her. She's down there three times a week. He's got these special prescriptions with her name printed on. She's getting her money's worth out of the NHS.

Mart Don't you go in with her?

Len Well I do, but I can't follow him. He says it's her age, wear and tear he says. None of us are getting any younger.

Mart You look all right though.

Len She can't sleep. Mind you, neither can I. She's up at two, wide awake. Pains in her chest and all the rest of it. Oh making my life a misery at the moment.

Mart Sounds like it's going to be a cheery weekend then.

Len At three o'clock of a morning I'm sat up at looking out of the window. I might as well be back at the pit.

Mart If there were any.

Len Oh ay, good point.

A beat

How's things then?

Mart All right.

Len How's teaching?

Mart Driving me mad. Half the students don't want to learn and half of them are too tired to listen. No it's not bad. I think I'm turning into a bit of a cynic.

Len How's this film thing?

Mart Still going on. They've told me to get a star.

Len Are they interested then or what?

Mart Well it takes time. I've been through three different companies. They say I've got to get a star interested. So I've sent it off to Tom Hanks.

Len Who's that then?

Mart He's a star. He won't do it but ——

Len So why have you sent it, if he won't do it?

Mart Dream world, Dad. It's all a load of blagging.

Len Ah, well then. Let's hope he likes it.

Mart I can't see it myself, but I'm going through the motions.

A beat

Len I never thought you'd end up teaching, you know.

Mart No.

Len I think it's a waste, I do.

Mart Yeh?

Len I mean you were a brilliant mimic as a kid, weren't you?

Mart No.

Len I always thought you should've used your talent for summat else. Like Jim Davidson or summat. I like him.

Mart I've got a Doctorate in English, Dad.

Len Ay, but I never thought it suited you, teaching.

Mart Anything else you think I should change about my life?

Len Well ——

Mart Go on, say it.

Len You do some daft stuff.

Mart I know.

Len She works for the film company then, does she?

Mart Yeh yeh.

Len Oh ay.

Mart It was just one of them things.

Len Oh right.

Mart I wondered when it might come up.

Len Well, you know what your mam's like about that sort of thing.

Mart I'm a sleaze ball then, am I?

A beat

Len Things can always be mended with April, you know.

Mart Can they?

Len I'm only saying.

Mart Yeh, I know what you're saying.

Len I mean, me and your mam have been through some rough times.

Mart I know that, I saw most of 'em.

Len No you didn't, you didn't see half of 'em. There were times many when I was going to leave your mam.

Mart And there are times now when you wish you had done, aren't there?

Len Well…

Mart Come on, Dad, you can't stay with one woman all your life, can you?

Len Well…

Mart Well I can't.

Len It takes some practice, I'll say that much.

Mart April was killing me.

Len That's par for the course. Your mother's killing me.

Mart Is she…

Len Oh she's getting awful at the minute. She always is when it gets near her birthday.

Mart It's not until Christmas.

Len Awful at the minute.

Mart Me and April — I dunno.

Len People have just got to get on with each other.

Mart Easier said than done in her case.

A beat

Len I can't understand you. You've got two smashing kids. I mean what did you want to be playing about for?

Mart I just wanted a change.

Len Bloody hell, what would it be like if we all thought that?
Mart Bedlam?
Len We'd be like a pack of wild dogs running about.
Mart Good fun though.
Len Fun, splitting a family up. You've got a queer sense of humour, you
have.
Mart Shit happens.
Len I know it's none of my business, but ——
Mart Don't spoil the weekend, Dad.
Len No...
Mart No, let my mam do that, eh?

Joan becomes animated once more US. *Mart and Len return* US *and sit*

The music stops

Joan Oh have you seen the muck on them curtains? I've just had a look out
of the back. It's grim out there. If you get lost out there you've had it.
Mart Yeh, you could easy get lost on them hills, get hypothermia and die.
Joan Listen to him, he's bloody ridiculous.

A beat

Mart Right well, what shall we do tonight, then?
Len Well, what do you want to do?
Mart Well, it's your break, what do you want to do?
Joan I don't want to do a lot.
Mart So what do you fancy?
Len I don't mind.
Joan I don't mind what we do, as long as we don't do a lot. I don't want to
be trailing about up here. I've seen in all the shops up here anyway.
Mart So, what is it that you want to do?
Len Well, I'm not bothered.
Joan No, I'm not.
Mart Well, shall we go out for a meal, or shall we stop in?
Joan When?
Mart Now.
Joan It's nine o'clock, I don't eat after nine o'clock.
Len We never eat after nine o'clock at home.
Mart Well, shall we have a drink?
Joan You don't want to be eating after nine o'clock, you can't digest your
food if you eat late. Do you normally eat late? It'd cripple me if I ate late.
Len We never eat late, do we?

Joan No, I don't fancy going out for a meal, not now.
Mart I can whip up a bit of pasta if you want? I've been to the supermarket.
Joan Your dad doesn't like pasta.
Len I do.
Joan You don't.
Len I don't mind it.
Joan It makes him badly.
Len It doesn't.
Joan Well you had an omelette at Málaga and that gave you a bubbly tummy though.
Len It did, I can't take omelette.
Mart Yeh, but what has that got to do with pasta?
Len I don't like omelette.
Mart Omelette's not pasta.
Len I like pasta.
Joan If your dad eats late it gives him the wind.
Len I'm like a brass band if I eat late.
Joan I don't know what it is, but it gives him the wind.
Len I had an omelette in Málaga.
Joan Talk about runs.
Mart Well at least it's something to talk about.
Len I don't know what they put in it.
Mart Egg.
Len I know there's eggs, but I don't know what they put in with the eggs to give me the runs. Runny egg, I think.
Joan He didn't know what they'd put in it, did you?
Mart Shall we body swerve this and talk about something else? There's a pub just down the road. We could pop down for a half?
Joan Oh no.
Mart It's nice. There's a karaoke, you'd love it, Mam.
Joan You go if you want, I can't go out after nine. If I don't go to bed early I feel badly the next morning.
Len If your mam doesn't get her sleep she's badly, aren't you?
Joan I'm badly.
Len She needs her sleep.
Joan I don't feel so well now to be honest. I feel like I'm going to have a funny "do".
Mart Are you all right?
Joan It's that bloody cold in here.
Len If she gets too tired she has a funny do. That could be bloody anything. You can't get to know what's wrong with her.
Joan I've got that spinning thing again.
Len Just sit quiet.

Joan I feel bloody awful.

Mart Is she all right?

Joan I've got that dizzy feeling again. You know, a tightness in my chest, and I feel light-headed.

Mart Is she all right?

Len She's been like this since we came back from Spain.

Joan I'll be all right.

Len Shall I get you a drink?

Joan Oh, your breath.

Len What?

Joan It's making me feel badly.

Len Look, are you ill or are you going to complain about my breath all night?

Joan Ah, it's disgusting.

Len You're supposed to be bad and all you're doing is going on about my blessed breath.

Joan You should've cleaned your teeth.

Len I'll take 'em out and let you clean the beggars if you want!

Joan Don't be so funny.

Len You're a blessed nuisance. She's like this every night.

Joan I told you I didn't like it up here. It's coming in on me.

Len What is it, is it indigestion or something?

Joan It could be.

Mart But you haven't had anything to eat. You say you don't eat after nine.

Joan I don't.

Len She had a bag of Maltesers when we were coming up.

Mart Why?

Joan Well I knew that you wouldn't be able to cook anything decent so I had to have something to take the taste of my tablets off.

Mart You had to have something to take the taste of your tablets off?

Joan They leave a funny taste in my mouth.

Mart Mam you should be on the telly.

Len She's right, I have to have a drink to take the taste of my tablets off, and then I have to have a piece of chocolate, to take the taste of the drink off.

Mart You're joking, aren't you?

Len No it's true. I mean I like fish, but if I eat it I've got to have a piece of cake after to take the taste of the fish off.

Mart I thought you liked fish though?

Len I do, but I don't like the taste in my mouth.

Joan Well you've never been any good at cooking. So I had to have something.

Mart So what you're saying is, it's my fault you've got indigestion?

Joan I said I didn't like being up here, you never know how long it's going to take you to get to the hospital.

Len Can you see what I have to put up with?

Mart (*to the audience*) So the next day, in the film script I call my life, we cut to an establishing shot of the Lakes. So we decided to take a boat trip across the Lakes to Ambleside. Of course my mam loves this.

Joan I hate boats. The last time I went on a boat we went on that trip to the Rhine valley with Sheila and Tom. Tom was sick five times.

Len That wasn't the boat ride. He'd had too much to drink.

Joan I think Tom had had an omelette.

Len Ay, I think he had.

Len and Joan walk DS. *They look at the imaginary lake. Mart is with them*

Lovely int it.

Mart (*to Len*) Told you, didn't I?

Len Int it lovely today?

Joan It always rains though.

Len It's not raining today, is it?

Joan It will do.

Len You always look on the black side.

Joan It always rains in the Lakes. It rained that time we went to Grange-Over-Sands in a caravan.

Mart Yeh, but that's not the Lakes.

Joan It's near though.

Len It's not raining today though, is it?

Joan Yet.

Mart (*to the audience*) A steamer pulls away from its moorings, people wave. My mam and dad are up at the front of the boat. Just stood watching. Smoke here, we need smoke.

Mart runs to the wings and picks up a smoke machine. He puts smoke around the legs of Jan and Len. He is creating the theatrical image

Blue sky, a fresh wind, spray from the Lakes, seagulls flying low, one shits on a woman from Crewe. She wins the lottery a week later, that's good, I think I'll use that. And I see my mam and dad stood lonely and lost, and for some reason I just stand watching them and I think that they are getting old. And I never even noticed. And my mind goes back to Blackpool, I'm nine and we're in the Tower ballroom.

Music plays: Begin the Beguine

Mart mimes the words and sings in slow motion

The smoke is now joined by a mirror ball, Joan and Len begin to dance around in the space. They are thirty years younger. They aren't bad dancers at all

It seemed so big, and they glided like they had no feet, and they were young.

Len (*to the audience*) Out on the dance floor I felt so alive. (*To Joan*) We're going to do all sorts.

Joan Are we?

Len We'll buy our own house, and go abroad, I'll get out of the pit.

Joan You should be on the telly you, you're bloody funny.

Len It's you who's the funny bugger.

Joan No you are though, kid.

Len I might go to night school.

Joan You?

Len I fancy being on the council, you know, do summat for the village.

Joan Ay they're all comics on t' council. Why don't you be a proper clown.

Len How?

Joan Be a politician.

Len I've got to be a politician, living with you.

Joan We can maybe have a week or two at Skipsea, when she arrives, you know?

Len I want another lad.

Joan We've got one. What do you want, a bloody football team? We'll have a little girl this time, and call her Susan.

Len Our Eddie's got a caravan, we can stay in that if we like.

Joan I gotta feeling you're foolin'.

Len No, I'm serious.

Joan (*singing*)   I gotta feelin' you're havin' fun…
                        I gotta go home when you are done.
                        Foolin' with me.
You're the best dancer in the Tower. Did you know that?

Len Yeh, if I didn't have two left feet I'd be laughing.

Joan Instead of being laughed at!

Len Very good.

Mart (*to the audience*) I remember that holiday because when we left the Tower I cried.

Joan Don't cry, what are you crying for?

Mart I cried because I'd seen a young girl with a calliper try and dance. I'd seen her struggle on to the dance floor with her mum and make pathetic movements with her legs. I saw the anguish in her face turn to joy as she mastered a few steps.

Joan Don't cry, Martin.

Mart My mam thought I was crying at them but I wasn't. She thought I was crying because the holiday was over and I was sad. But I was crying at the spirit and the helplessness of the human predicament. Funny how that moment has stayed with me. Funny.

Len Right, who wants fish and chips?

Joan Me; do you want some, Martin?

Len Who wants mushy peas?

Joan Not you. Please!

Len We'll be there for you, Martin.

Joan We'll see to you…

Len You'll be right with us…

Joan Have you grazed your knee? Come on, let me have a look at it.

Len Just don't tell lies, remember that, kid.

The mirror ball effect ends

Mart (*to the audience*) Have you got kids? I've got two girls. Martha, two and Frieda, four. Not my names, April's. April's not my name, either. April's my wife's name. Well ex-wife. Well she's not even my ex-wife, we're still married.

Len I wish you'd have brought the kids. They'd've enjoyed the boat trip, don't you think, Joan?

Joan Well I didn't, I hate boats.

Len I could've told 'em about knots, you know. I ——

Mart (*to Len*) Ay and bored them to death.

Len I know a lot about knots. I read a book about knots once. Don't know why but I just read it. I saw a book about tying knots and I read it. It was only second-hand but ——

Mart That must be where my literary side comes from!

Joan It's always damp up here. No matter how sunny it is. It's always damp.

Mart It's not damp, Mam, it's currently eighty degrees, in fact it's the warmest day they've had in the Lakes for the past twenty years.

Len I love boats. I could buy a boat. If I ever won the lottery I'd buy a boat.

Joan Where would you keep it?

Mart (*to the audience*) The *Wordsworth Coffee House*. It's one of the nicest in Ambleside and I decide that I'll treat 'em to an omelette and a bag of Maltesers. Close three shot of us sat in the corner.

Len Nice in here.

Mart Funny how Wordsworth's name was also what he was. Like he wrote words, of worth. Isn't that weird? I've often thought about my name. Dawson. That must mean I'm the son of a door.

Joan Is there a toilet?

Mart (*to Joan*) Why, do you want to go?

Joan No. I just wanted to know if there was a toilet.

Len I think there is a toilet.

Joan I don't want to go. I just wanted to know if there is one.

Len Shall I ask?

Joan Is there one?

Mart Yes, I think they do have toilets in the Lakes. And of course, if there isn't one you can always go in the lake.

Len I think there's a toilet, there must be. All restaurants have got to have a toilet nowadays, haven't they?

Joan Well, you never know.

Mart Right, what's anybody want?

Joan Well, I'll make do.

Mart With what?

Joan With nothing.

Mart You can't make do with nothing.

Joan I don't like what they've got on the menu.

Mart You haven't looked yet.

Len Yes. Yes. Over there.

Mart What is it, another comet?

Len Over there, I've spotted the toilet.

Mart So what do you want, Dad?

Len I'm not bothered.

Joan Your Dad dunt like eating out.

Len I'll have a pot of tea.

Joan They never cook the veg enough for him.

Len Is there a pot of tea?

Mart Don't you fancy a bit of braised steak, or some soup. Baked potato?

Joan Oh don't bother about us, Martin, we'll make do.

Mart Well why didn't you say you'd make do before we came in?

Joan I'm quite happy to make do, are you love?

Len Oh ay, I'll make do, I will.

Mart (*to the audience*) Now you see this is the thing. I could see other happy families talking and enjoying their dinners, having serious and meaningful discussions about the new government, and whether Lottery money should be used to fund hospitals, and should we re-introduce the death penalty for pinching bread. But me? My family need to know that there is a shit-box in the restaurant, not that that they actually want to use it, but they just want to know that it's there. Which is I suppose the kind of reassurance you need when your bladder starts to play up. And they are happy to "make do", like millions of their generation. They make do with a pot of tea and a cream cake. It's so *frou-frou* it's crucifying. Watching them in that coffee house was like watching Chekhov done badly. No no, I'm wrong. It was like watching a Brian Rix farce done in Hebrew!

Len I can't go to the toilet when I'm out anyway. I'm getting awful.

Joan He's getting awful.

Len Can't go for days sometimes.

Joan Thank God!

Mart (*to the audience*) I'm going to write the Martin Dawson guide to restaurants. Marco Pierre White's in London doesn't get five stars. It gets a star for a pot of tea and a three shitehouse rating.

Joan Fancy doing that?

Mart (*to Joan*) What?

Joan Embarrassing us in there.

Mart Well it's a restaurant, Mam, you go in and order food, that's what you do. You can't sit there with a cup of tea, there's a minimum service charge unless you want sixty-seven pots.

Len It wasn't our kind of place anyway.

Mart Well, what do you want to do? Shall we go and get some tripe and sit in a cow pat and have a picnic?

Joan He thinks he's funny.

Mart It's not me, it's you.

Joan Oh, he's off.

Mart No, sorry. OK. Sorry. I've forgotten it. Let it go. There it's gone, forgotten. I will wander lonely around the shops as a cloud.

Joan Don't start off on one of your bouts because your dad can't stand it.

Len I'm all right.

Joan He says he is, but his angina gets to him. If you get him worked up it sets him off.

Mart Are you all right, Dad?

Len It gets to me now and again.

Joan I mean, I'm driving him mad so he doesn't want you playing up.

Len Yeh, I mean we haven't come up here for an argument. have we?

Mart No, course not.

Joan We could have had one of them at home.

Len It just gets to me you know, I don't want any hassle.

Joan He's always showing us up.

Mart I thought we were going to forget it?

Len You know. I wake up some mornings and I still think it's time to go to work. I stand there thinking, Now I've got up for something, what is it that I've got up for? I've got up for something. And then when I think of what's happened with the pits, that gets me.

Joan That gets him, it's a funny thing but that gets him.

Len It's your emotions, you see?

Joan We'll have a look around the shops then, shall we?

Mart I thought you hated the shops up here?

Joan Well, we've come all this way...

Mart You bugger!

Joan Come on, I might get myself a cardigan.
Len I don't know why she bothers, she always takes 'em back.

Len exits

Mart (*to the audience*) So, I'd got this screenplay to finish. It was being developed by Blue Lobster Films. They've made one or two low budget features and they think my film has promise. So then I met Tilly. Ah man. Tilly's tits were something else. Can I say tits? They were something else. And she wants me to change my script. Listen, for those tits I'd change my life. Well I did. Anyway we're working close together, you know what I mean? And she's bright. Double first; I didn't know that women like that existed. I should've seen it coming. I was flavour of the night I think. I mean, she's off now shagging somebody out of *The Thin Blue Line*. And I didn't really have to tell April, did I? I mean, most men don't. Oh come on, be honest. Most men have the odd one and they don't tell a soul, they carry it around like a golden medal. Like it's the kind of thing you only get out and look at in the showers or on the back seat of the rugby bus. But I can't keep it all in. Maybe I wanted it to happen to upset April, maybe I needed it to shock me back to life.

Mart goes to join Joan

Joan He's just gone to take one of his tablets.
Mart (*to Joan*) How're you keeping then?
Joan Don't upset your dad.
Mart I'm not, am I?
Joan He worries about you.
Mart I'm fine.
Joan You've changed, haven't you?
Mart Aren't you getting a cardigan?
Joan Can you hear me?
Mart No, I've suddenly gone deaf.
Joan Fancy running off with somebody called Billy.
Mart Tilly, Mam, do me a favour. Get the name right at least.
Joan You'll come a cropper, you will.
Mart It's just one of those things. Everybody's at it. I'm surprised you're not at it with the milkman.
Joan Was April?
Mart Not as far as I know.
Joan Well that's two of us who aren't at it then. And I think you can count your dad as a third.
Mart He's taking his time though, you never know.

Joan It takes him forever to do anything nowadays.

Mart He could be popular then.

Joan Don't try and change the subject.

Mart Listen, I'm thirty-six in August. I'm a bloke.

Joan I know that.

Mart Don't you get tired of having a go?

Joan No. You've changed and you won't admit it to yourself.

Mart I haven't.

Joan I don't know if it's April and her mother or those at work or this bloody Tully woman.

Mart That's all finished. And why shouldn't I change. What will it say on my tombstone. Martin Dawson, he never changed?

Joan Never changed his underpants that's for sure.

Mart That's not bad.

Joan I don't know.

Mart What did you expect me to do? Not change? You wanted me to marry Claire Sewerby, didn't you?

Joan She was nice, was Claire.

Mart Yeh, but she was crippled in a car accident when she was twelve, wasn't she?

Joan She's still a nice lass.

Mart I'm not saying she isn't.

Joan She was a lovely lass was Claire, and she always liked you. God knows why!

Mart It must be my charm.

Joan What charm?

There is warmth and a laugh between them

Len enters

Len What a bloody carry on. I dropped my reading glasses down the toilet.

Joan What were you doing on the toilet?

Len What do you think I was doing?

Joan I thought you went to take a tablet?

Len I did, but once I've had a drink I've got to go.

Mart Why didn't you go in the restaurant?

Len Ah, because I'd not had a drink.

Mart You had a drink of tea.

Len Tea doesn't do it to me. I've got to have a cold drink.

Joan So what were you doing with your reading glasses?

Len Sat reading.

Joan Sat reading?

Len I had a shit and all!

Music plays softly under. Music plays to set them out of the scene then fades for the next dialogue

Have you enjoyed it?

Joan I'm tired out, and my ankles are killing me.

Len So you've enjoyed it, then?

Joan There's nowt to look at really. There's just them little trinket shops.

Len Summat to do.

Joan I wish he'd got the kids, we could've played with 'em. I saw that playground I thought, well we never see 'em, do we?

Len I've enjoyed it.

Joan I mean fancy leaving them with Pam and Donald? I bet he never sees 'em? He'll never see 'em now, will he? You know what she's like.

Len Ay, I've enjoyed it.

Joan And our Martin looks shocking. He looks worse than me.

Len Well it's all book work int it?

Joan He looks pasty. I bet he gets no bloody fresh air.

Len Well, he has today.

Joan He looks shocking to me. He's going bald and all, did you see that?

Len I was bald at thirty. Mind you, that was being with you.

Joan It's a wonder I'm not bald being with you!

Len He's all right.

Joan What's this script he's doin' about then?

Len I don't know. I don't like to ask too much. He might take my head off. I think it's called "Battered".

Joan Is it about a fish shop?

Len It could be.

Joan It's probably about having an affair, he can't hold his own water.

Len Listen who's talking.

Joan Fancy.

Len Ah well.

Joan The little sod, him.

Len It's his business.

Joan Mind you I never liked April. She was so bloody posh. It was like meeting the bloody Queen. And Pam? Good grief. What do they think they're doing? I just couldn't get on with her.

Len You don't get on with anybody though you, do you?

Joan Ah look, I told you.

Len What?

Joan Rain. It's raining.

Len Ay, you said. Raining.

Joan It's raining, Martin. I told you it would. It always rains. Everytime I come to the Lakes, it rains.

Mart You came thirteen years ago, didn't you, with my aunty Mabel?

Len And it rained every day.

Joan He thinks he's funny.

Len He is.

Mart (*to the audience*) I looked at them, sat on the boat, on the boat going back. They were like two stones rubbing together. They thought the same, spoke the same, they were meant for each other. For better or for worse. And it was then that I had the thought; I will kill them both before they return to Doncaster on Sunday.

Joan Look at his face. I said it would rain.

Len She was right.

Joan I said it was going to rain.

Len Murder the weather up here, though, isn't it?

Mart (*to Len*) It is, isn't it?

Joan Look at him, he's got that mischievous look on his face.

Mart Have I?

Joan He had that look on his face when him and Robert Jones broke the kitchen window.

Mart The woman remembers everything. It's scary.

Joan Oh Martin, what's happened to you? Where's the little lad we had who used to laugh at everything. He never laughs now, does he?

Len Never laughs.

Joan He never laughs now!

Len Ay, he's always been an outsider.

Joan All his life.

Mart Most murderers are though, aren't they?

Joan What?

Len What's he say?

Mart Raining. Bloody typical, you said it would rain, didn't you?

Joan It must have followed us up from Doncaster.

Len Like a big black cloud.

Mart (*to the audience*) I could do it. I knew I could. I would push my mam over the side of the boat. She couldn't swim and my dad would have an angina attack.

Joan Do you come up here a lot then?

Len She hates the Lakes.

Joan Hate 'em.

Mart You see, they are so different from Pam and Don. I'd actually forgotten how different they were. April's parents are witty and erudite, learned and sensitive. Pam's an actress, RSC, sit-coms, all of that. Don's a QC. Has trips abroad, a villa in Perugia, he's got a pen with his initials on it even.

Joan Are you from the south? We hate the south, don't we?

Len Hate the south. We think we ought to declare war.

Joan There's only one good thing come out of the south.

Len Ay, the train to Doncaster!

Mart And that's another thing, they talk to anybody who'll listen. They went to Rome ten years ago and were sat talking to a statue until the police moved them on.

Len and Joan begin to talk to imaginary punters on a boat

Joan Just for a few days.

Len He was up here by himself, renting a place, so ——

Joan This is our son, Martin. He's a lecturer.

Len Thirty-six in August.

Joan Only he's writing a film for Tom Jones.

Len Hank Marvin! Hank Marvin, isn't it?

Joan He's been writing it for years.

Len He's got more degrees than a barometer.

Joan So we thought we'd come up and join him.

Len She doesn't like the Lakes.

Joan Martin does though, loves it up here. I don't like the Lakes.

Len She doesn't like the Lakes.

Joan No, we didn't vote, did we?

Len Waste of time.

Joan Waste of time, he says.

Len By the time they change anything, we'll not be here anyway.

Joan We didn't vote, well he hurt his leg at war.

Mart And she's off, my mother is now talking absolute bollocks!

Joan They said they wouldn't close the pits, but ——

Mart You need a degree in linguistics to keep up with her.

Joan But they're not bothered. So we shop in Sheffield most of the time now.

Mart My wedding? A nightmare. My mam and Don only spoke two words to each other. Hallo, so long.

Joan When was the strike now?

Len I was made redundant after the strike.

Joan Hurt his leg bad, and the union…?

Len I'd always been a Labour man, but ——

Joan We never got a thing during the strike, did we?

Mart Don told me he couldn't understand what she was saying.

Len The union took that long…

Joan But it's the same with the council, all out for themselves.

Len They all are.

Joan He used to be on the council, but ——

Len Packed it in, didn't I?

Joan He's a Doctor aren't you, Martin?

Mart I laughed at her.

Len Oh ay, he's a Doctor. Not of medicine.

Joan I wish he was. I've been feeling bloody awful lately.

Mart It's like being in a Beckett play.

Joan We didn't vote this time, but there's a sale on at Marks and Spencer's in Doncaster, but his dad ran a garage, didn't he?

Len Everybody's out for themselves. I'm not big on politics. But that's what it is today, politics, politics, politics.

Joan He says that they're all the same.

Len They're all the same to me.

Joan But his brother ran a garage, didn't he? He was hit by the Mother's Pride van in the Asda car park at Carcroft. Backed straight into him, didn't it?

Len Crushed him.

Mart Don said it was like talking to an imbecile.

Joan Straight into him, and he'd been in the Green Berets, so it just goes to show you!

Mart So I'd decided if I was going to kill them, that I'd kill my dad first.

Len And he was in the Green Berets. Wasn't he?

Mart It's his fault that my mam's like she is. He's let her get like this. I'll hide his angina pills. That's what happens in my screenplay. Tom Hanks takes his parents out to Long Island and he kills them. He can't bear to see them grow old. I'm going to kill mine because they bore me to death!

We are off the boat and back in the cottage

Len So what are we going to do tonight then? Shall we watch *Match of the Day*? I always like watching Liverpool. I don't support 'em, but I like to watch 'em.

Mart (*to Len*) You don't fancy a pint down the pub, then?

Len Well your mam's about had it. It's not fair if we go out, is it?

Mart Well, shall we have a glass of wine? I've got a load of stuff in special for you coming up.

Joan Oh, don't bother about doing anything special for me, Martin.

Mart Have you enjoyed it then?

Joan Well we've done nowt, have we?

Len I've enjoyed it.

Joan We've just sort of pottered about.

Mart You've had a look around the shops.

Joan I didn't buy owt though. I had a look at a cardigan ——

Mart For an hour ——

Joan There's no shops to call owt. And I said it'd rain, didn't I?

Len Everytime your mother comes to the Lakes it rains.

Joan It must be me.

Len It must be.

Mart Well I'm sorry about the fact that it's raining. In fact I'm beginning to feel sorry that I invited you up here in the first place.

Joan Well.

Mart Because whatever I do it will not be right for you.

Joan I didn't want to come, I told you that.

Mart The moment you arrived.

Joan That's the trouble with him now. You can't talk to him.

Mart Mother you don't talk to anybody, you attack them.

Len She attacks me.

Joan Well if I can't speak my mind to my own son, it's a bugger.

Len Your mam's always been straight to the point, you know that.

Joan He's been with that lot for that long.

Mart Who's that lot?

Joan April's lot. You know who I mean. They're that bloody prissy if somebody spoke the truth to 'em they'd have a bloody stroke.

Len Well, they are a bit different.

Joan It's them and us, and it always has been ever since the wedding.

Mart Who are you then, Richard Hogart?

Joan I don't know why you couldn't have come and stayed at our house.

Mart You're joking aren't you? I'd've never got any work done for you hoovering up!

Len She doesn't do as much as she did.

Joan I mean if she's kicked you out …

Mart She hasn't kicked me out.

Len It's her father's house anyway, isn't it?

Mart We're paying him back.

Len I wouldn't have had that.

Mart He bought it for us.

Len No, I wouldn't've had that. I told your mother at the time. That's no way to carry on. Politics. You're in his pocket, aren't you?

Mart Let's just leave it, shall we?

Joan You started it off.

Mart Are you going to leave it?

Joan You started.

Mart Are you going to let it go or are we going to say some things that we're all going to regret?

Joan Well if you've got something to say that we might regret, if that's the way you're thinking, you'd better come out with it now.

Mart So you've got some things to say that I might regret, is that what you're saying?

Len You'll not beat your mother, kid, you never have.

Joan He's not getting the better of me, he thinks he's bloody clever, I'll show him who's clever.

Len Now let's laugh it off, the pair of you.

Mart Do you want to laugh it off?

Joan Do you want to laugh it off?

Mart Do you want to laugh it off?

Joan Do you?

Len Now let's leave it, you two.

Joan Do you want to laugh it off, or are you going to go on?

Mart Look at the pair of you. You're as good as dead.

Len The way you're both going on I will be.

Mart You're just like the whole lot of your generation. Fed on *Countdown* and *Coronation Street*. Your life's a pantomime. What do you look forward to?

Len Nothing really.

Joan We did look forward to seeing the kids, but you can't keep your trousers on. So that's put paid to that.

Mart Nothing.

Len There is nothing to look forward to at our age.

Mart So why complain about everything?

Joan He'd have been better off if he'd've got a job at Curry's like Marjorie Black's lad. He's the manager now in Bawtry.

Len He was always a nice bloke was Nigel Black.

Mart (*to the audience*) You see the thing is about those types. You know, our mams and dads? The old working class? The old Labour, if you like? What do they do, eh? The retired? The redundant? The distinctly uneducated masses that make airlines their millions. The half a lager and a rum and black brigade? The two weeks in Benidorm and a caravan at Cayton Bay set? The, "Well we like to walk to the garden gate and count the buses" lot? What use are they now? Their life has been lived, but they blame you for living yours. This great splodge of grey power, what shall we do with them? I have my own idea. I think at sixty, you should take an exam. Call it the "sixty plus", if you can't answer a few simple questions, and turn a caravan into your driveway. "Termination time." Kill 'em. I mean look at Pam and Don right, they are the same age as my "m" and "d" but what a difference. Money makes a difference. But what do my "m" and "d" do now? Well they trail around the shops, trail to Spain and sit in Spanish hotels surrounded by other English people who're old and grey and brown, with wrinkling, handbag leather skin, and they do the slosh with retired miners from Durham, endlessly repeating "Scargill was right" like a mantra. Oh and they collect naff Lladro statues which they think are beautiful. They travel, but they don't see anything. They're so guarded, so narrow minded, and the worrying thing is, they want to take my kids and fill their heads with the same bile, the same lack of vision that they fed me with.

Joan We like Spain.

Len We went to Mijas didn't we?

Joan Bought our Martha a little bull.

Len Lonnie Donegan lives in Mijas.

Joan It's pronounced Mihas, isn't it?

Len Mihas.

Mart And they call in at the *Yorkshire Lad* or *The Saddleworth Coffee House* because they do real English tea, but with real Spanish milk. But they can get a full English breakfast twenty-four hours a day. Then their tubes get clogged. And half the clientele have got heart problems anyway, but they stuff in the sausages, and dip their egg with fried bread. Talk about "chips with everything".

Len It's lovely up Mijas, isn't it? (*Pronounced, "me arse"*)

Joan He's like one of them, him.

Len One of what?

Joan You know, like when you go to the doctor's, and you can feel them looking down on you. They just haven't got time for you.

Len Ah well.

Joan He's not bothered what we think.

Mart (*to Joan*) I'm sorry, there's a lot of things I shouldn't've said.

Joan Too late now. Mind you, I bet he has a good laugh at our expense when he's with April's mother. And I'll tell you this, I don't like that sit-com she's in. I think it's rubbish.

Len I don't watch it.

Joan She didn't speak two words to your aunty Mabel at the wedding.

Len Mind you, that's no bad thing.

Joan Not two words.

Len Neither did I.

Mart You what? I'm sure they're not bothered what you do.

Len I think we've had enough of this tonight anyway.

Joan We'll go early in the morning.

Mart Fine.

Len Joan?

Mart OK, if that's what you want to do, fine. In fact, why don't you go now?

Joan Let's go now then.

Len I can't drive in this lot, it's bloody throwing it down out there.

Mart Look, I'm sorry, I didn't want this. I didn't want this, honest. I'm up here. I'm on my own, I didn't want this honestly. I didn't want us to fall out. Mam, Dad, I wanted us to have a good time.

Joan You never come and see us.

Mart Honestly. I don't want this. Let's do what intelligent people do ——
Joan We're not intelligent though, are we, according to you.
Mart Can you let it go?

Joan is becoming emotional and will be in tears through the next speech

Joan We're bloody nobodies according to you. I wish we'd've just left you, I do. I told your dad, I said, let's go up and see our Martin. This is before you actually asks us. I said, let's go and give him some support. It must be difficult for him, and this is what we get, this is what we get. We're not well and we come to support you.
Mart I know, I don't want this.
Joan It's so bloody awful. I wish I'd not come…
Len E dear…
Joan He's making me badly he is — my nerves are all over the shop. I worry about him and my nerves are all over the place.
Mart Oh Jesus.
Joan I can't stop here.
Mart Mother. Mother. Listen.
Joan I knew it'd be like this.
Len Her nerves are bad, you know. You didn't have to go on about Mijas, did you?
Mart It didn't mean anything, did it.
Len It's the only bit of pleasure she gets.
Mart I didn't mean anything by it.
Len So words are meaningless! That's rich coming from you.
Mart I need you, at the moment. I need to, Jesus. Can't you see? I'm lost here. I need you, can't you see that. Can't you see beyond your own fuckin' problems?
Len No need for that blessed language is there?
Joan I feel bloody lousy. I mean she always thought she was marrying beneath her, didn't you see that at the wedding?
Mart I know that now.
Len Let's go to bed. We'll go to bed, Mart. She'll be as right as a bobbin in the morning. Come on. We'll go to bed, and then we'll get off early. It's not just you.
Joan It's not me. It's not me all the time. It's him and all. Tell him, you never say anything to him, you think the sun shines out of his bloody arse.
Len I've had this since we got back from Spain.
Joan It's not me. It's not me all the time.
Mart Why are we arguing?
Joan Shit.

Mart OK, if you want to hear it. Everything you said about April was true. But I've stayed for the kids, Jesus. I stayed with her for the kids.

Len Let's let it drop now, can we?

Joan He'll be the death of me, he will. He'll be the death of me.

Joan and Len sit frozen. They are lit by overhead spotlights

Mart (*to the audience*) So it's Saturday night. Mam and Dad cried their way to bed. Wonderful. I was thinking of asking them up here every weekend. A bottle and a half of Oxford Landing later and I'm just beginning to feel myself again. Suddenly banging from aloft.

Len Turn it down. We can't sleep for that noise up here!

Mart Tomorrow, what will it be? Sunday roast and, "I don't like my veg done like that." And what about when we went to Malta? And "Have you seen that girl with a stud in her lips?" So I decided that, that night, I would put my dad's tablets down the bog.

Len Martin, turn it down a bit.

Mart He can hear the wind blowing outside. (*To Len*) I can't do a thing about the wind, can I? You should know that.

Joan It's a bit cold up here.

Len Can you put that fan heater on for your mam? She's a bit cold up here!

Mart I'll come and set fire to the bed, shall I, that'll warm her through!

Len Go to sleep, Joan.

Joan I feel bloody awful.

Mart (*to the audience*) So I put the fan heater on. I put it at full. She'll be like a crisp in the morning.

Joan All this upset, I can't stand it.

Len Just relax.

Joan I'm sweating like hell.

Len Just try and get to sleep, love.

Joan That heater's bloody warm.

Len We can't tell him to turn it off, can we?

Joan My heart's racing...

Mart So I thought, I could suffocate them both. Get a pillow.

Joan I've got awful pains, Len.

Len It's your arthritis, love...

Mart Push it over their faces.

Len It's arthritis love. Go to sleep, love, go to sleep.

Joan Oh Len, I feel bloody awful...

Len I don't feel well myself.

Joan Oh, my... oh hell.

Mart They'd struggle a bit, but ...

Joan Get a doctor.

Len Are you OK?

Joan I need a doctor.

Mart And the weather is just right.

Joan I need to see a doctor!

Mart She said it would rain.

Joan Get our Martin.

Len (*banging*) Martin! Martin!

Joan Oh hell, this is it…

Len Martin! — I'm in agony myself — Martin … !

Mart (*to Len*) What?

Len Martin?

Mart What's up?

Len Your mam's not so good.

Mart What is it this time, is she too warm?

Len I think she's having a heart do. Can we get a doctor, kid? I'm sorry to bother you. I know you're trying to work. But do you think you could get your mam a doctor?

Mart (*to the audience*) It's like she's haunting me, like she's always with me. I mean when I lost my virginity my mother was sat in the corner of the room knitting our Susan a bobble hat.

Joan is having a heart attack. Mart looks at her and makes no effort to help her. The Lights fade on Mart. The music swells

ACT II

The House Lights fade

Mart bounds back on stage into a spotlight and immediately begins his routine once more

Mart So we're in the hospital, right, I've had a bottle and a half of red wine and I am desperately trying to keep it together. I think I hit three cars getting there. I had to swerve to miss a nun. It was either a nun or a giant penguin. I mean can you credit it? I'm all revved up to kill my parents and suddenly my mam has a heart attack! I mean, talk about bad timing. We walk into the hospital and I'm staggering about that much, the doctor thought it was me that was ill. It's like bedlam in there. Two o'clock Sunday morning and we're still in Casualty. My mam's laying behind a nylon screen, which needs a good wash. I did some shadow puppets on it for her, but it didn't cheer her up much. And my dad's wandering around the waiting-room like he's lost his senses...

Len enters. He walks around for sometime trying to get comfortable. Then he sits. Mart comes to join him

(*To Len*) All right?
Len Oh dear.
Mart Calm down.
Len I'm still shaking. I can't stop shaking.
Mart Just relax.
Len You're the worst driver I've ever been in with.
Mart Hey, I could hardly see, we're lucky we got here at all.
Len I bloody know that. How we missed the lorry was a bloody miracle.
Mart God moves in mysterious ways.
Len You're gunna have such a headache.
Mart I have already.
Len It's lucky we didn't get arrested.
Mart We're here, aren't we?
Len I nearly had a stroke.

A beat

Mart Have you had an angina tablet?
Len Yeh.
Mart Just sit and relax.
Len I can't.
Mart You'll have to.
Len Oh look at us. What a weekend.
Mart Just stay calm.

A beat

Len I knew one day it would come to this.
Mart Come to what?
Len Well, you never say the things you need to say, do you? Always putting 'em off. You never think that day'll come.
Mart Which day?
Len This day.

A beat

Mart My mam says what she needs to say.
Len So do you.
Mart Yeh well.
Len I'm not making a point of it here, but there was no need for all that earlier.
Mart Leave it, Dad, eh …
Len There was no need for it. That's all I'm saying. There was no need for it.
Mart I've heard you, three times now.
Len Bloody ridiculous.
Mart Are you saying I set this off?
Len Well it can't have helped, can it?

A beat

Mart That fan heater wouldn't have helped, would it?
Len It was all dry air.
Mart Do you think that caused it then?
Len It must have been ninety degrees in that bedroom.
Mart Oh shit.
Len You and your antics.
Mart This is awful.

A beat

Len I hope she's all right.

Mart So do I.

Len I've never really told her how much she means to me.

Mart Well she knows that, doesn't she?

Len I try to tell her but, you know what she's like. She keeps telling me that she doesn't need to be told.

Mart That's my mam.

Len It's not her who needs it, though is it? It's me who needs to tell her.

Mart Bertolt Brecht never told his mother he loved her, and when she died it was too late.

Len Gordon Baines told me the same thing.

Mart What, about Brecht?

Len No, about his mother.

Mart Yeh, right, yeh.

A beat

Len So do you think she'll be all right?

Mart I dunno.

Len Do you?

Mart I don't know.

Len I think she will be, do you?

Mart Dad, what can I say?

Len Well you're a doctor, aren't you?

Mart Yes, but unless she pops up and suddenly wants an essay on modern theatre marking, I'm in exactly the same boat as you.

Len You feel so bloody helpless, don't you?

Mart I mean, I was never any good at biology. I thought a fibia was a Roman lie.

Len Pack it in.

Mart I can't help it, it's a disease. Maybe I should get treated while I'm here?

Len I think I'll go and have a walk outside.

Mart It's still throwing it down out there.

Len I can't stay in here, it's all coming in on me.

A beat

Mart I feel bloody lousy.

Len Your mother? She always has to have something happen to her. Look at when you were born; she had to have a blood transfusion. It's never straightforward is it? I mean what are they doing in there? Nothing. As far as we know she could be dead.

Mart Dad!

Len Well, we don't know do we?

Mart (*to the audience*) So we're there, like Hamm and Clov talking about anything from a gnat's bollock to Tony Blair's haircut. I mean, when I wanted them dead, I didn't mean dead dead. We were there about an hour when a Spanish doctor comes to see us. He's not a Doctor of Spanish, he's a doctor who is Spanish. Mind you he's not a heart specialist either, he's a stomach man. I'm a tit man myself, but you know all about that. He's the only one available to talk to us. My dad stood listening to the doctor, pretending he understood what he was talking about. Juan Carlos wouldn't have understood what he was talking about.

Mart becomes the Spanish doctor. His English is so poor it is almost impossible to understand what he is saying

(*To Len*) Hella Meesta Doorsoon?

Len Dawson.

Mart So. We luok at your wiffe.

Len Yes yes.

Mart Maybe a problum.

Len A problem?

Mart Maybe. We don't knoe. So we luok.

Len You don't know?

Mart So perhaps we do thrlee test.

Len Three?

Mart We see if she has had a heart hattacht.

Len She's had a heart attack ?

Mart We luok…Si.

Len At her heart?

Mart We do thlree.

Len Three?

Mart Si.

Len Three heart attacks?

Mart Si thlree.

Len She's had three heart attacks, has she?

Mart We do some test.

Len On her heart?

Mart Thrlee test.

Len Will she be all right?

Mart We do some test.

Len She'll be all right, won't she? What did he say? I couldn't follow him proper?

Len exits. Mart returns to his act

Mart (*to the audience*) You know, half an hour earlier I was in there with my mam having an ECG done when three kids jump into her cubicle shouting and bawling. They'd stabbed their mate up the arse with a chisel, and had gone down to Casualty for a laugh. Completely out of their heads. I mean, I was pissed, but these guys were flying. Whoever works on Casualty needs a medal, right. Or even better. More money. Give them all the money you've got. "Get your fuckin' money out now." The woman in the cubicle opposite my mam was brought in from a local asylum. She'd been pulled out of bed, by her eyes! Hey, this is the truth here. She's squealing in agony, poor sod. And the bloke in the cubicle next door, who is eighty-seven, hasn't been to the loo for two months. It sounds like he's got a frozen breezeblock up his arse. So they've given him a laxative. Sounds to me as if they need semtex. The whole thing is straight out of a Kafka. It makes *ER* look like *Tots TV*. I'm there with my mam, who I've obviously killed, helping the staff nurse try and get the ECG machine to work, and the only thing I can think about is how do you make this funny!

Len re-appears. He is much more anxious now

Len Spanish doctor's been again. He says the consultant won't be on until the morning. There's a leg man but he's no good. He's a stomach man. And the liver man's off with a bad foot. I've just had a look at her. She dunt look well.

Mart (*to Len*) Dad, she's had a heart attack. What do you expect her to do, cart-wheels?

Len Do you think we should tell our Susan?

Mart Well, she's in Florida, she can't do a lot about it, can she?

A beat

Len She was right, you know.

Mart What?

Len She told me she felt unwell when we went up Mijas. I just ignored her but she told me she felt queer. That's where we bought that donkey for Martha. Must have been the hills. She said she wasn't well and I trailed her around there like a pack horse. I mean I can't carry the bags myself either, can I?

Mart You've got to go away though, haven't you?

Len I mean, to be honest, I only half listen to anything she says.

Mart (*to the audience*) Now, I don't know if it's an inbuilt safety valve, but suddenly me and my dad start performing as if my mother is already dead. For some reason we suddenly fast forward six hours. And begin to mourn her passing.

The Lights change

Len sits and is very distressed. Mart hovers uncomfortably

The music plays under the scene, gradually fading

Len Oh dear.
Mart (*to Len*) Don't.
Len I don't know what to say.
Mart There's nothing you can say, is there?
Len Look at us! What's she doin' in there eh, with all that bloody lot?
   Headbanger drunks. Bloody idiots smashing each other's bloody heads in!
   What's she doing with all that bloody trash? She never did anybody any
   harm, you know?
Mart I know…
Len I don't know what I'm going to do with the house.
Mart You don't have to do anything yet, do you?
Len Sell it.
Mart Where are you going to live?
Len Well I can't live there, not without your mam.

A beat

   I never got to know her, you know?
Mart Course you did.
Len No I didn't. I mean we never get to know anybody really, do we? I mean
   deep inside. We're always alone. We're always going through life on our
   own. It's just that now and again we need a bit of a leg up. I wanted to get
   to know her, but she wouldn't let me near her really.
Mart She wouldn't let anybody near her.

Silence

Len Oh I did some daft things and all, you know?
Mart We all do.
Len I mean early on. I got involved.
Mart Well — anyway.
Len She never knew. I felt like a bloody louse.
Mart Dad?
Len I couldn't tell her, could I? Three years it went on. And I loved her. Well
   I thought I did.
Mart Dad, leave it.
Len So different, isn't it?

Mart Oh ay.

Len Goor three years. I never said a word. I mean, I don't know if she knew or what? I didn't know which way to turn either. She'd had you.

Mart Forget it.

Len She worked in the Co-Op this woman. I used to go and see her and then come home and take you for a walk.

Mart Oh right.

Len God I've kept this quiet for thirty-five years.

Mart Bloody leave it.

Len I'd look at you and cry over what I was doing. Was it wrong, Martin?

Mart Don't ask me.

Len I wish I'd've told her.

Mart Why, it would've killed her.

Len I've lived a bloody lie.

Mart Forget it.

Len What a bloody mess, eh?

Mart Oh, Dad, man. You pick your moment.

Len Oh ay, and she wasn't the only one.

Mart Eh?

Len There were three other women after her and all. I mean I couldn't leave 'em alone.

Mart Bloody hell, man.

Len I must have had this animal instinct or summat?

Mart Good grief …

Len Any chance I'd got and I was at it. Eh, what am I?

Mart Well I … ?

Len A bloody animal.

Mart And me mam never … ?

Len She never knew. There was the woman from the milk. The woman from the Post Office and Betty from the flower shop.

Mart No wonder we had a house full of bloody flowers.

Len Goor eh, they things we do, eh? Pathetic, isn't it?

Mart Sounds bloody impressive to me if you want to know the truth.

Len Human failings eh, kid? Human failings.

Mart (*to the audience*) So my dad's giving me all this stuff and I swear I felt as if I was going insane. I mean I'm still bloody tipsy. I'm not sure if what he's saying is true or if he's making it up. I mean hospitals make me feel unreal anyway. And suddenly my dad's in the psychiatrist's chair, and I'm the psychiatrist. Oh yes it all came out, their names, where they lived, when he used to see 'em. It turns out that the daughter of the Co-Op one was the girl I'd lost my virginity to behind Theakers' pig farm, sixteen years later. Weird eh? What did I say about my life being a film?

Silence

Len You could have come with us, you know.

Mart (*to Len*) Where to?

Len The *Angela*?

Mart I know, but ——

Len She said it would be her last holiday and she was right, poor lass! It wouldn't have killed you, would it?

Mart No.

Len Too busy in London, eh?

Mart You know what it's like.

Len I do.

Mart What would you have rather done?

Len No comment.

Mart Well then.

Len It's a nice hotel, the *Angela*. You would've been able to just sit and watch us dance. You used to enjoy that.

Mart I used to wet the bed and eat coal and all.

Len They have a "happy hour" you know! Two drinks for the price of one. Yeh, they could have done you a good deal, hundred and fifty nine quid half board!

Mart (*to the audience*) We're acting as if my mam's dead and my dad's turned into a rep for Lunn Poly. He's giving me the hard sell on the holiday of a lifetime. But you see that's what that weekend break was all about. It was all about me not going to Spain. It was about guilt. Mine, not theirs. But I'd already told my mother… No!

Joan enters, dressed in a different outfit. She is quite well here. We are eight months earlier

Joan Why don't you come?

Mart (*to Joan*) I can't, I'm in London that week.

Joan Fly out from Gatwick. You'd love Maurice and Carmen, wouldn't he?

Len You'd love Maurice and Carmen. They're on every night. He plays and she sings. They're brilliant, aren't they?

Joan They always wave at us when we go, don't they?

Len We've been to the *Angela* sixteen years on the trot.

Joan They always wave at us Maurice and Carmen, don't they?

Len She sings in Spanish. They do the macarena! They do that lambada don't they?

Joan They do the lambada, don't they?

Len They do, don't they?

Joan Come on. You might as well come. Bring your computer, you can do some work while you're there.

Mart I can't.

Joan You can.

Mart I've got some work on in London.

Joan Course you can!

Mart Well, actually, I don't want to!

A beat

Joan Oh right.

Mart It's not really my thing. Beside Pam and Don are talking about having another bash at theirs. And I've already promised the kids. I think Ant and Dec are going to be there, they've booked a clown and all sorts. You ought to come down, you know; they have invited you anytime!

Len No, it's not our scene, is it?

Joan Oh well, you do what you like. But we like it, don't we? We like it.

Mart continues his routine

Mart (*to the audience*) I didn't want to sit and watch them do the slosh. I didn't want to watch them dance for two minutes before they got too tired and had to sit down. My dad sweating and gasping for breath. My mam's face red from too much sun and high blood pressure. I didn't want to watch them demonstrate their oldness. I didn't want to be reminded of their demise. I knew what a week in Spain would be like. It was like a weekend in the Lakes. Only worse. It would be all about them reminiscing about all the good times. Can you remember when...?

Joan walks into the stage and picks up the action. She then disappears once more. They both sit on chairs US, *half lit*

Len We went to Blackpool and he was seven, can you remember?

Mart When he did this...

Joan What about when he dropped that crazy golf club through the pier?

Mart When he did that...

Joan And you had to wait for the tide to go out before you got your deposit back?

Len What about when we went on that boat in Stanley Park, and the engine packed in?

Joan We were out there for three hours.

Len Come in number sixteen, your time is up.

Joan Talk about laugh.

Len Come in number sixteen, your time is up.
Joan Number ninety-one, are you in trouble?
Len Talk about laugh!
Mart It would have been like being on *This is Your Life*, for a week!
Len Can you remember when he was in the school play?
Joan Can you remember him lying to us about his first girlfriend at school, and then us finding out who she was?
Len Yeh. Yeh I can.
Joan He's always been a little fibber!
Len Yeh yeh, he has.
Joan I don't know where he gets it from.
Len Neither do I!

Joan exits

Mart Oh no, I didn't want any of that. I wanted to be talking film. I wanted to be talking Bertolucci, Wim Wenders, Tarantino, Mike Leigh. I wanted to be talking art. I really wanted to be taking Tilly from behind and watching my face in the mirror above her bed. I wanted the excitement of rolling around naked in bed with a young woman who thought I was a genius. Well, she did!

Music: Mario Lanza, The Donkey Serenade

Mart stops his routine and goes off stage

Mart enters, he brings on a large hospital bed. The bed is painted black so only the body of Joan stands out. Len helps him bring the bed on. As he does this Mart speaks over the music

Now I never expected to do this. I thought they'd fly this in for me. But it's all a part of the *verfremdung* effect. Right so, close two shot right. Hospital. Four thirty a.m. My mam's on her way out.

The music fades. Len sits by the side of the bed. The atmosphere is extremely tense

Len I'm here.
Joan Tired.
Len Just relax.
Joan My ankles are all swollen up.
Len Yeh.
Joan Oh hell, Len...

Len I know.

Joan Oh hell.

Len I've spoken to the doctor.

Joan Nice bloke.

Len Yeh yeh. I can't understand him though.

Joan No, neither can I.

Len Bloody hell.

Joan They're doing their best.

Len That's right.

Joan The ECG machine was broken, they had to send for another one.

Len Just sit quiet.

Joan Our Martin's got to get private health, tell him.

Len That's right.

Joan I'm frightened, Len.

Len I know.

Joan I'm really frightened.

Len You just shut your eyes and relax.

Joan I can't, I've still got palpitations. I'm really scared, love. I don't want
to die.

Len You're not going to, are you?

Joan They're on about shutting this hospital.

Len Just lay quiet.

Joan They've been good to me. He's a nice doctor.

Len If you could understand him.

Joan You never think it's going to happen to you, do you?

Len No.

Joan And then…

Len looks over Joan

Len Do you want a drink or anything?

Joan Oh your breath!

Len Don't.

Joan Have a mint if you're talking to the doctor.

Len It must be my stomach nerves.

Joan Oh dear.

Len Just…

Joan Have you got some mints?

Len I'll get some.

Joan Good grief.

Len Sorry.

A beat

Joan Make sure you do the brasses, won't you? And look after the garden.
Len Just relax.
Joan And I owe Lucy Jackson thirty quid for the flowers on my mam's grave.
Len Joan?
Joan Make sure she gets it because I was late paying last time. And all the stuff in the loft has got to go to our Susan. And pay the milkman, will you.
Len Why where are you going?
Joan This is it. I can feel it.
Len Just — be quiet.
Joan Yeh?
Len Yeh.
Joan I'm so tired.
Len I know.

Len holds Joan's hand. Music: Mario Lanza, Beloved!

The music swells through this entire next sequence which should have the feel of film. Mart sits at the side of the stage, takes out some popcorn and begins to watch his life as if it was a film. Len holds Joan's hand. She lays still. He looks at her. He is crying heavily. He turns away and walks away from the bed. He is sobbing

Joan All right?
Len Yeh yeh.
Joan Sit down, love…
Len I'm all right. Just feel like I've got a cold coming on.
Joan The weather.
Len That bloody cottage of our Martin's!
Joan He can't do owt right.
Len It's not like Spain, is it? It's not hot, is it?
Joan Bloody damp makes my arthritis play me up.

Len blows his nose. He is a little more composed now, and he returns to Joan's bedside. He looks at her and then sits

Len I — er ——
Joan Sit down.
Len I can't settle.
Joan You're getting on my bloody nerves.
Len I've done some daft things, you know?
Joan We all have.
Len I — er — you know did some daft things years ago.
Joan Not now, Len.

Len I was fair to you, you know.
Joan Please, love …
Len I mean, there's been others, kid. Shit.
Joan Please, love …
Mart (*to Len*) What are you doing, you silly gett?
Joan Other what?
Mart Forget it.
Len I just want you to know that …
Joan So tired.
Mart Say it …
Len I — er ——
Mart Tell her you love her!
Len I don't want anything to happen to you.
Joan Neither do I! Is he sober?
Len Not quite.

Mart steps in to the scene. The music fades under

Mart (*to Joan*) All right, Mam!
Joan You!
Mart You're in the best place.
Joan Your bloody driving!
Mart Got you here though.
Joan If I ever get out of here I will swing for you.
Len (*still emotionally upset*) She's a bugger.

Len leaves the hospital room. But he is still on stage. Mart sits at the bedside

Mart They'll get you sorted.
Joan Yeh?
Mart Course they will.
Joan I bloody hope so.
Mart Yeh.
Joan If anything happens, keep an eye on your dad. He's bloody useless without me.
Mart (*to the audience*) My mam tried to sleep, but the bloke in the next cubicle was still wailing and trying to have a shit, he was trying so hard it was making me feel dizzy.
Joan Tell him to throw all the stuff out of the fridge and all.
Mart (*to Joan*) I'll tell him.
Joan Cold in here now.
Mart I'm sorry for putting the fan heater on, Mam.
Joan I wish he'd stop shouting next door.

Mart Yeh, he's making me feel bad.

Joan When we went to the *Angela,* Maurice and Carmen played our favourite, you know?

Mart Did they?

Joan I would've liked to play with Frieda and Martha.

Mart You hate those names, don't you?

Joan You should have called them Sandy and Samantha.

Mart Sandy and Samantha? April would have had a fit. She said they were too down-market, and I agreed with her. If she walked in here now I would batter her brains in with a fucking big brick.

Joan We only wanted a bit of what everybody else gets.

Mart Mam, just relax, this is not doing you any good.

Joan I bet she stopped you from coming.

Mart Mam?

Joan I bet she did.

Mart No, she didn't.

Joan I bet she did.

Mart Mam?

Joan We only wanted to re-live some memories, me and your dad.

Mart walks DSR

Mart (*to the audience*) Cut to me outside and I'm having a fag. More kids are brought into the hospital, broken noses, black eyes. A little baby who won't stop crying. A bloke in his eighties whose stomach ulcer has burst. And I think, bloody April. I've always taken notice of April, and bloody Pam and Don. From the moment I first met them I was impressed by their money, by their accents, by their jobs, by their friends, by their furniture. I mean fancy basing your entire life plan on somebody else's furniture? I must be going mad. And Pam is so bloody smug when I come to think about it. She's in that awful sit-com "Home and Hearts". I could write better stuff than that. I could write better stuff than that sat on the bog with my arm up my fuckin' back.

Len comes back to the bedside

Joan He should've never married her.

Len Let it rest.

Joan They were never suited.

Len Just leave it, please leave it. Just give it a miss.

Joan I told you at the time.

Len How're you feeling?

Joan They weren't really suited.

Len Can't you let anything go?

Joan I mean, why did he have an affair with a twenty-three year old?

Mart Oh come on, you don't have to be a brain surgeon to work that out, do you? Mind you I didn't have to tell April either, did I? "What?" she says, in that kind of over-dramatic, almost unbelievable, way. "What?" I've been unfaithful. When I was in London. "How many times?" Why what does it matter? "How many times?" Well quite a few. "Right, go, just go" Stop shouting! "You make me sick!" I don't know why I didn't apologize but I didn't. I just stood there. The kids were crying. April was going mad. And then she really wheeled out the big guns. "You're so insecure, you're so unsure of yourself, the first person to show any interest in you and you go off with them. You little little man. You've got an inferiority complex. What do you do? You teach theatre studies to students who don't care if all the theatres in the world burnt down tomorrow. You're constantly trying to prove yourself, and you don't know who you are." The kids are running round by then, they think we're playing. I think Frieda knew something was going on. I mean, I knew there'd be payback time. I knew as I was laid in Tilly's arms that there would be payback day. There's always payback day. It's like Newton's third law. To every action there is an equal and opposite reaction.

Len comes DS *to Mart*

Len Doctor's in with her, kid. Can you have another word with him? See what's what!

Mart (*to Len*) I will, but unless you want a bottle of San Miguel and some sun cream, I'm snookered.

Len You talk to him.

Mart How is she?

Len She's asleep.

Mart Right.

Len What a bloody do!

Mart Ay.

Len Poor old lass.

A beat

Don't ever, you know.

Mart Oh no.

Len You know. I've said it and that's it. It had to come out and there we are.

Mart Come here.

Mart gives Len a big hug

Len Get off.

Mart I love you, Len.

Len Ar well?

Mart I love you. I didn't think I did, but I bloody do.

Len What for, doing what I've done?

Mart No, for just being my dad.

Len Bloody hell.

Mart Sorry, I didn't mean to.

Len Ah well. I wouldn't want it everyday like, but I quite enjoyed it!

Mart Once every thirty-five years is enough for you, is it?

Len Easily enough.

Mart Oh I dunno, I done some daft things, Dad.

Len I know that.

Mart No, not just with Tilly. I mean that was always going to be short-lived.
I mean with you and my mam.

Len Ar well.

Mart I've shut you down, haven't I?

Len I don't know what's been going on this last couple of years. It's all
bloody changed. Me and my angina, your mother's nerves. You just
seemed not to be there for us.

Mart I know.

Len And our Susan being in Florida doesn't help.

Mart I think I'm lost, you know? I think I'm a bloody weakling to be honest.

Len No you're not...

Mart I am. I'm stuck. I'm only writing this bastard film to try and impress
Pam and her friends. And suddenly when I started doing it April said she
wanted to act.

Len You're not a weakling, kid. You just don't know what you want.

Mart Does anybody?

Len Well, we make do.

Mart I mean I've been daft with Pam and Don.

Len Well, they're famous aren't they? I mean I've seen him on that
Newsnight. Different world, int it?

Mart Ay, and I thought it was better.

Len It is, make no mistake about that.

Mart I don't think it is.

Len Come on, waken up, you don't want to be like me and your mam, do
you? Scrating and saving. Bloody money makes the world go around. I told
your mother I could understand what had happened. You'd seen how the
other half lives, and it's not a bad old life, is it?

Mart Everything I've done over the last five years I've done to try and
impress Pam and Don.

Len No, you haven't.

Mart I have, I have. In fact I've tried to impress everybody all through my life.

Len You didn't have to impress us. You're just our Martin to us.

Mart I even lied about you and my mam to them.

Len Ashamed of us, are you?

Mart I must have been.

Len Bloody hell.

Mart I was just ashamed of what you did. I was scared of what they might think about you.

Len I'm not bothered.

Mart I thought that they'd judge me through you.

Len I'm not bothered what anybody thinks about me. They can shit for me. This is me. I can't be any different.

Mart I used to pretend you didn't go away because I knew what they'd say about the sort of holidays you had. I knew what they'd say if I told them that you'd been to a caravan site at Cayton Bay.

Len No they're not like that, are they?

Mart I had a discussion with Pam once. I was still at university. I told her I loved my mam and that I didn't want to go away from home.

Len So what's up with that?

Mart She told me it was immature and that love didn't exist.

Len Arseholes.

Mart Dead right.

Len I can't follow 'em, me, I can't honest.

Mart We were around the table one night at Don's and Pam's and he was talking about infidelity. He said Pam could sleep with whoever she wanted and it wouldn't affect him. It was her body and she could do whatever she wanted with it. He said that people are too possessive over each other.

Len What did you say?

Mart I asked if I could take Pam upstairs for a fuck! I mean she's not in bad shape, you know?

Len A chip off the old block, eh?

Mart No I didn't, but I thought about saying it.

Len Thinking it's bad enough.

A beat

Mart I hope she's all right, Dad.

Len Ay. So do I hope she's all right.

Music: Mario Lanza, Song of India

Mart (*to the audience*) So we're stood talking, right, and I have this sudden *gestalt*. This flash forward twenty years! We're in exactly the same situation. My mam's eighty-nine and it really is it this time. I haven't seen them for ages. I go into the hospital room and my mam's on a life support thing. My dad can hardly walk.

Mart walks over to the bed. Len has gone over to the bed. He sits. The music fades

(*To Len*) All right, Dad?

Len Ar.

Mart Not so good then?

Len They've changed her. All she does is fart now. I've been rubbing her legs, but I don't think she can feel owt. Nowt bloody left in her now.

Mart Na.

Len How's the kids?

Mart Fine fine. Martha's at UCLA now, doing a film course. Frieda's at the RSC.

Len I saw her in them adverts.

Mart Yeh?

Len Very good.

Mart Pam got it her before she died.

Len Ay, I heard about that. Gang rape, wasn't it?

Mart Awful.

Len Targeting the rich, weren't they?

Mart It's crippled April.

Len Ay, I bet it has. Bloody hell. What's the soddin' world coming to, eh?

Mart I dunno.

A beat

Len How's teaching?

Mart Same as ever.

Len Still not heard owt from Tom Hanks then?

Mart No… I've got an interview next week for another job in Leeds, but…

Len Should've got out of teaching…

Mart Oh ay, it's that easy.

Len stands. Joan has died. There is no emotion

Len I think she's gone, kid.

Mart Yeh.

Len I think she's gone.

Mart I should've killed her, Dad.

Len No.
Mart I should've killed you both.
Len Life's too precious.
Mart What sort of life is it though?
Len Life's precious kid. You should've lived it.
Mart What you going to do?
Len Oh, I'll go back home and sit and look out of my window. Got a lovely little rockery you know? Lobelias and daffs and all sorts!
Mart I'll see to things here then.
Len Cheers, kid.
Mart Where's our Susan?
Len She's been here for the last five nights. She was having tonight off. I'll go and give her a call. Tell what's gone off!

Mart walks DS *to where he was. Len freezes where he is near the bed with Joan on the bed, after her death*

Mart (*to the audience*) I should've done it, you see? It would have saved them twenty years of utter embarrassment. Her not able to walk. Him wheezing and gasping like an old sofa. I should've pushed them off that bloody boat. I just didn't have the bottle. I didn't have the bottle to do it! I should've done it, but you see that's the conundrum. I don't like prisons. So it was a question of killing them and spending the next twenty-five years locked up and guarding my rear, or of putting up with their mindless rantings.

Len becomes animated. He comes urgently down to Mart. We are now back in the present

Len Martin, heart man's been. He says your mam's OK.
Mart (*to Len*) Eh?
Len He says she's OK. He says she must have had a spasm or something. Could have been a virus. Fibulation or summat. She can come out. She's just getting dressed. Oh you should see her, she's nearly back to her old self.
Mart Never.
Len Oh ay, she seems right as rain!
Mart Oh well.
Len Aren't you pleased?
Mart Course I am!

Joan enters

Joan Len? Len? Come on, let's get off. It's like a bloody nuthouse in here. And I want a bloody word with you. Drinking and driving, stinking of ale, doing bloody silly shadow puppets, you're a soft as a brush. How you ever got to teach is bloody beyond me.

Mart I might pack it in anyway.

Joan His whole life's a bloody joke.

Len Your mam, eh?

Mart Wonderful.

Joan And what were you on about in there?

Len When?

Joan When I didn't feel so well. I thought you wanted to tell me something?

Len Oh, you know me, I don't know what I'm on about half the time.

Joan Yeh, that's what I thought. I thought, look at me, I'm on my last legs and all he can think about is his bloody self. Come on then!

Len Your mam's back, kid.

Mart Yeh, just like Arnie.

Len Oh yeh, she's back!

Music: Donkey Serenade

Joan and Len exit. The bed is struck. The music fades

Mart (*to the audience*) So I'd lost three stones in weight worrying that I'd killed my mother, wondering how I'd cope with penal servitude. Wondering whether I'd be treated with respect in prison or whether I'd be the whipping boy for some giant from Essex, and it turns out at the end of the day she's all right. She's had a virus. A virus. I mean she could have at least have had a heart attack. I mean, I used to have to work with a virus. Now look, I don't know what kind of relationship you have with your parents, and frankly 'cos, if I've been nothing else, I've been frank here, I don't care a fuck. All I know is, I was happy to see the back of them. I love 'em, et cetera., they're a great old couple, etcetera. They've got their funny side, et cetera. But to be honest, that was the worst weekend of my entire life. And I thought, so what that they love *Countdown* and *Coronation Street*. So what that my dad had never read Balzac, and that my mam didn't use a wok and eat foreign muck. I was just happy for them to do whatever they wanted in their house in Doncaster, as far away from me as possible. In fact I was so delighted to see the back of them, I went and paid and booked for them to have a holiday to get over the weekend. Two weeks in Los Boliches, full board. I know, I know, I need serious psychiatric assistance.

Joan enters. She is dressed in holiday clothes. Len enters. He also wears sun clobber

Joan I love Spain.

Len Oh ay.
Joan And we're not doing anything this holiday.
Len No.
Joan We're going to no Mijas. We're just going to sit in the sun and relax.
Len We are.
Joan We bloody are.
Len We are.

Joan begins talking to an imaginary couple

Joan Hallo, are you from the south? We hate the south, don't we?
Len Hate the south. We think we ought to declare war.
Joan There's only one good thing ever come out of the south.
Len Ay, that's the train to Doncaster!
Mart (*to the audience*) Now I hate flying, you know that. But I'm up in the Lakes. April's not talking. Blue Lobster Films told me they couldn't raise the cash for my film. Not even if we had Tom Hanks, Hank Marvin, Tom Jones, Marvin Gaye and Tammy Terrell or the Pope playing my mam. Films about parents were a non-starter apparently. Why didn't they tell me that when I went to see them? Not enough sex and drugs in it apparently. Not enough drugs? Come on, my dad's full of 'em. And sex? Look no further than our family. Sex, *moi*! So I phoned Tilly, but she was out of the country with a bloke who did adverts, he does that pan cleaner one. Talentless bastard. I could have thought that one up. And then to top it all, to top it all, April phoned me and told me she'd just got a part in a new Mike Leigh film. Pam had got it for her. I wouldn't mind but she's not even an actress.

I've got this bastard film script and nobody but nobody will do it. The only other interest I'd got was from Channel Four Film Shorts and even they wanted to change it. "Could we make them an Irish couple?" they said. I said no, and then I knew what I'd do. I'd do it as a stand-up. Then it was all mine, nobody would interfere with it.

So I thought, sod it! I'll go away and write it as a stand-up routine. Right. Sod it. I booked on a flight, and took my two little girls to see their gran and grandad in Spain. April had a fit! You should've seen Pam's and Don's faces when I told them we were going in a tent to Benidorm. Pam looked like she'd shit her pants! And as we left their house, I said "So long" to Don, I'd wanted to say that since the wedding. We got the last room at the *Angela*. We stayed there a week, we danced, played on the sands, went up Mijas. It nearly killed my mam. We had sausage and chips in the *Yorkshire Lad*, with loads and loads of tomato sauce, and I got rat-arsed one night on

Boddington's in the *Saddleworth Arms*. It was a laugh. It was a brilliant laugh. I mean it was awful as well but it was a laugh. I didn't do a stroke of work that holiday, I just sat and watched my mam and dad play with my kids. And I laughed, I laughed until I cried.

And then it struck me. Pam and Don never laughed. I had never seen them laugh, not a laugh right from the bottom of their souls. Not an up Mijas laugh. Not a laugh that made your ribs ache. Not a laugh like you were having a heart attack! People like Pam and Don never laughed like that. I know that for a fact, I'd been to the theatre with them. We went to see an Ayckbourn and they didn't laugh once, and at the end of the night they said it was hilarious! Hilarious? They had no idea what was hilarious.

That week in Spain was, without question, the worst week's holiday I had ever had, but my two little girls loved it. They loved it that much we've booked to go again in September. I told you I was mad, I mean I still hate flying. Well, you've been an audience. I've been many things, I used to be a lecturer in drama and now I'm trying to be a comic. Some say there's no change. Thanks for listening. I did think of finishing with a song, but I'm a shit singer. So I'm going to finish with a dance, and I'm a shit dancer. Good-night.

Maurice and Carmen play the Lambada

Mart begins to dance the slosh. It is both surreal and strangely good

Len and Joan join in with him and both begin laughing

The Lights fade on them

FURNITURE AND PROPERTY LIST

ACT I

On stage: Two black dining chairs

Off stage: Small travelling bag (**Len**)
Small bag (**Joan**)
Smoke machine (practical) (**Mart**)

ACT II

Off stage: Large hospital bed painted black (**Mart**)
Popcorn (**Mart**)

Personal: **Len**: handkerchief

LIGHTING PLOT

Practical fitting: mirror ball

Please note that the additional use of the spotlight during **Mart**'s act is left at the discretion of the lighting director

ACT I

To open:	House Lights and preset fade to black-out	
Cue 1	Doctor Martin Dawson (**Mart**) enters *Bring up spotlight on* **Mart**	(Page 1)
Cue 2	**Len** appears US *Bring up spotlight on* **Len**	(Page 2)
Cue 3	**Joan** enters *Bring up general lighting*	(Page 3)
Cue 4	**Joan**: "And my feet …?" *Cut spotlights. Bring up general lighting*	(Page 3)
Cue 5	**Mart**: "… her ears bleed, or something." *Dappled gobo to create lakeside garden*	(Page 7)
Cue 6	**Mart**: "No, let my mam do that, eh?" *Bring up general lighting*	(Page 10)
Cue 7	**Mart**: "… we're in the Tower ballroom." *Snap on practical mirror ball*	(Page 13)
Cue 8	**Len**: "… remember that, kid." *Cut mirror ball effect*	(Page 15)
Cue 9	**Joan**: "He'll be the death of me." *Bring up spotlights on* **Joan** *and* **Len**	(Page 28)
Cue 10	**Mart**: "… our Susan a bobble hat." *Lights fade on* **Mart**	(Page 29)

ACT II

To open: House Lights fade. Bring up spotlight on **Mart**

Cue 11   **Len** enters   (Page 30)
             Cut spotlight. Bring up general lighting

Cue 12   **Mart**: "And begin to mourn her passing."   (Page 34)
             Lights change

Cue 13   **Mart**: "… mother … No!"   (Page 37)
             Lights change

Cue 14   **Joan** and **Len** sit US   (Page 38)
             Half lit effect on **Joan** *and* **Len**

Cue 15   **Len** and **Joan** join in the *Lambada*   (Page 51)
             Fade to black-out

EFFECTS PLOT

ACT I

ACT II

A licence issued by Samuel French Ltd to perform this play does not include permission to use the Incidental music specified in this copy. Where the place of performance is already licensed by the PERFORMING RIGHT SOCIETY a return of the music used must be made to them. If the place of performance is not so licensed then application should be made to the Performing Right Society, 29 Berners Street, London W1.

A separate and additional licence from PHONOGRAPHIC PERFORMANCES LTD, 1 Upper James Street, London W1R 3HG is needed whenever commercial recordings are used.